# You Smashed It!

summersdale

YOU SMASHED IT!

Copyright © Octopus Publishing Group Limited, 2026

All rights reserved.

Compiled by Maria Medeiros

No part of this book may be reproduced by any means, nor transmitted, nor translated into a machine language, without the written permission of the publishers.

Condition of Sale
This book is sold subject to the condition that it shall not, by way of trade or otherwise, be lent, resold, hired out or otherwise circulated in any form of binding or cover other than that in which it is published and without a similar condition including this condition being imposed on the subsequent purchaser.

An Hachette UK Company
www.hachette.co.uk

Summersdale Publishers
Part of Octopus Publishing Group Limited
Carmelite House
50 Victoria Embankment
LONDON
EC4Y 0DZ
UK

This FSC® label means that materials and other controlled sources used for the product have been responsibly sourced

www.summersdale.com

The authorized representative in the EEA is Hachette Ireland, 8 Castlecourt Centre, Dublin 15, D15 XTP3, Ireland (email: info@hbgi.ie)

Printed and bound in China

ISBN: 978-1-83799-779-4
eISBN: 978-1-83799-780-0

Substantial discounts on bulk quantities of Summersdale books are available to corporations, professional associations and other organizations. For details contact general enquiries: telephone: +44 (0) 1243 771107 or email: enquiries@summersdale.com.

To..................................................

From..............................................

**You don't have to be great to start, but you have to start to be great.**

Zig Ziglar

Success is liking yourself, liking what you do and liking how you do it.

— Maya Angelou

# A LITTLE PROGRESS EACH DAY ADDS UP TO BIG RESULTS

**One step at a time, I get to make positive choices to fulfil my dreams.**

Deena Kastor

# The first minute of action is worth more than a year of perfect planning.

## James Clear

**Your victory is right around the corner. Never give up.**

Nicki Minaj

Celebrate the person you are becoming; you are worth every step

**Identifying the pattern is awareness; choosing not to repeat the cycle is growth.**

Billy Chapata

**BELIEVING IN YOURSELF WHEN NO ONE ELSE DOES – THAT MAKES YOU A WINNER RIGHT THERE.**

Venus Williams

# YOUR WINS ARE VALID, NO MATTER WHAT SIZE

> Each small victory, even if it is just getting up five minutes earlier, gives you confidence.
>
> Arnold Schwarzenegger

# You've always got to believe in the positives.

Lewis Hamilton

# THE SMALLEST OF ACTIONS IS ALWAYS BETTER THAN THE NOBLEST OF INTENTIONS.

Robin Sharma

Show up and do the best for yourself no matter what the situation

You can make whatever you want of your life. If you want to get somewhere, you can get there.

Davina McCall

# Don't let anyone tell you what you can and can't do or achieve.

Emma Watson

**Simply by trying – you become the hero of your own story**

I didn't get there by wishing for it or hoping for it, but by working for it.

**Estée Lauder**

> Don't judge each day by the harvest you reap but by the seeds that you plant.
>
> Robert Louis Stevenson

# If you've got nothing else, passion will get you through.

## Henry Cavill

Give yourself credit for the days you've made it when you thought you couldn't

**As hard as it is, owning who you are and knowing what you want is the only sure path to affirmation.**

Ashley Graham

**Success is often achieved by those who don't know that failure is inevitable.**

Coco Chanel

**GOT UP,
DRESSED UP,
SHOWED UP**

> You are strong enough to handle your challenges, wise enough to find solutions to your problems and capable enough to do whatever needs to be done.
>
> Lori Deschene

> **Vulnerability is not weakness; it's our greatest measure of courage.**
>
> Brené Brown

You are worth the investment; show up for yourself every day.

Samantha Davis

Your dreams turn into plans when you turn a "can't" into a "can"

**Change your life today. Don't gamble on the future, act now, without delay.**

Simone de Beauvoir

**If you follow your bliss, doors will open for you that wouldn't have opened for anyone else.**

Joseph Campbell

Being comfortable in your own skin is priceless

You are
never too
small to make
a difference.

> Greta Thunberg

**There are ups and downs, but whatever happens, you have to trust and believe in yourself.**

Luka Modric

**It's important to be fearless yet vulnerable. It takes courage to do both.**

Nicole Scherzinger

It only takes a minute to shift your energy, set the tone of your day – to make changes for the better

# Know what you want and reach out eagerly for it.

Lailah Gifty Akita

> The dictionary is the only place that success comes before work.
>
> Vince Lombardi

Don't wait for opportunities – go make them

**If you think you're being met with resistance, that probably means you're doing something new.**

Taylor Swift

**Be messy and complicated and afraid and show up anyways.**

Glennon Doyle

**Overpower.
Overtake.
Overcome.**

Serena Williams

# SLOW DAYS OVER FAST RESULTS

**History has shown us that courage can be contagious, and hope can take on a life of its own.**

Michelle Obama

**If my mind can conceive it, if my heart can believe it, then I can achieve it.**

Muhammad Ali

The door to your next level is open – it's time to walk through it

**Write it in your heart that every day is the best day in the year.**

Ralph Waldo Emerson

Define success on your own terms, achieve it by your own rules, and build a life you're proud to live.

Anne Sweeney

I've learned it's important not to limit yourself. You can do whatever you really love to do, no matter what it is.

Ryan Gosling

# CELEBRATE YOUR MOMENT NOW – DON'T WAIT FOR LATER

Success isn't reserved for the chosen few. It's built by the ones who develop the right habits and do them daily - long after the excitement wears off.

Dean Graziosi

As you get small wins in life, you have to integrate those wins into your identity and know that you're a strong person.

Brendon Burchard

# Feeling the fear but moving forward regardless makes you a winner

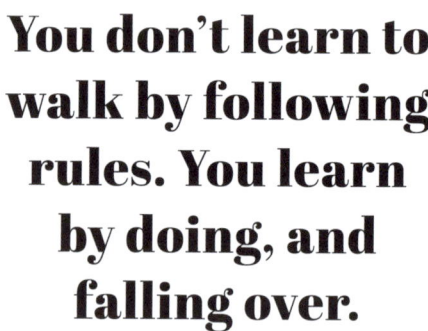

**You don't learn to walk by following rules. You learn by doing, and falling over.**

Richard Branson

**Stay afraid
but do it anyway.
What's important
is the action.**

Carrie Fisher

**SOMETIMES YOU CAN HAVE THE SMALLEST ROLE... AND STILL HAVE A BIG IMPACT.**

Neil Patrick Harris

If you are wise enough to know when you need help and brave enough to ask for it – that deserves applause

**Life is a series of natural and spontaneous changes. Let things flow naturally forward in whatever way they like.**

Lao Tzu

**There are no regrets in life, just lessons.**

Jennifer Aniston

# SMALL STEPS EACH DAY WILL LEAD TO BIG CHANGES

# If you cannot do great things, do small things in a great way.

Napoleon Hill

**All progress takes place outside the comfort zone.**

Michael John Bobak

You don't have to be perfect to achieve your dreams.

— Katy Perry

**SHOULD**

**WOULD**

**COULD**

**DID**

# I try to start every day and end every day by taking a moment to be grateful.

Olivia Wilde

I feel very confident that the ideas that I have, however big or small, will finally find its place in the world.

Frieda Pinto

# No one can do what you do exactly the way you do – that's your superpower

**Show up for yourself and believe in yourself and you'll be amazed at what you can achieve.**

Alan Young

**IF YOU HAVE A DREAM, FIGHT FOR IT.**

Lady Gaga

> The only way of discovering the limits of the possible is to venture a little way past them to the impossible.
>
> Arthur C. Clarke

Celebrate your victories because no one understands what it took to accomplish them

**Be your own definition of amazing, always.**

Nikita Gill

# We are often the change that we seek.

Barack Obama

Recognize where you are today and how hard you've worked to get here

# I attribute my success to this: I never gave or took any excuse.

Florence Nightingale

**Perseverance is a great element of success.**

Henry Wadsworth Longfellow

Courage starts with showing up and letting ourselves be seen.

— Brené Brown

# Every achievement starts with the first step - the decision to try and to follow through

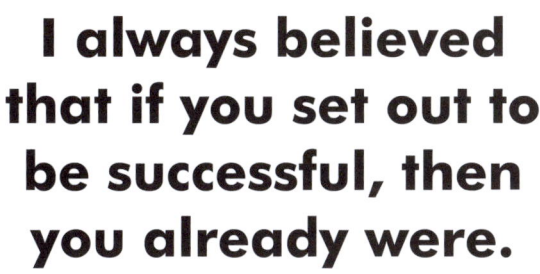

**I always believed that if you set out to be successful, then you already were.**

Katherine Dunham

**YOU CAN CARVE YOUR OWN PATH, BE YOUR OWN KIND OF LEADER.**

Jacinda Ardern

# LOVE YOUR PRESENT, TRUST YOUR JOURNEY

Life comes with many challenges. The ones that should not scare us are the ones we can take on and take control of.

Angelina Jolie

**Action is the foundational key to success.**

Pablo Picasso

**Start where you are, use what you have, do what you can.**

Arthur Ashe

SMALL STEPS STILL MOVE YOU FORWARD

**If you can do what you do best and be happy, you are further along in life than most people.**

Leonardo DiCaprio

**Don't watch the clock; do what it does. Keep going.**

Sam Levenson

SEE THE BIGGER PICTURE, FREE FROM JUDGEMENT

> To accomplish great things, we must not only act, but also dream; not only plan, but also believe.

Anatole France

The first step toward success is taken when you refuse to be a captive of the environment in which you first find yourself.

Mark Caine

**At the end of the day, we can endure much more than we think we can.**

Frida Kahlo

Knowing when to leave, whatever the situation, takes courage – be proud of yourself

Be grateful for the progress you are making, no matter how small.

— Anonymous

# I was smart enough to go through any door that opened.

Joan Rivers

**You are stronger than any challenge, more powerful than any obstacle**

If you can't fly then run, if you can't run then walk, if you can't walk then crawl, but whatever you do you have to keep moving forward.

Martin Luther King Jr

Know when to laugh at yourself, and find a way to laugh at obstacles that inevitably present themselves.

Halle Berry

**You alone are enough. You have nothing to prove to anybody.**

Maya Angelou

YOU SHOWED UP - THAT ALONE IS ENOUGH

**Great things are not done by impulse, but by a series of small things brought together.**

Vincent van Gogh

# Enjoy the journey of life and not just the endgame.

**Benedict Cumberbatch**

# Cheers to tiny achievements! They all add up

I am learning every day to allow the space between where I am and where I want to be to inspire me and not terrify me. I can even ask for help!

Tracee Ellis Ross

The more you praise and celebrate your life, the more in life there is to celebrate.

Oprah Winfrey

**Today's accomplishments were yesterday's impossibilities.**

Robert H. Schuller

# EMBRACE YOUR JOURNEY, EVERY STEP MATTERS

**Success isn't about the end result, it's about what you learn along the way.**

Vera Wang

**Once you choose hope, anything's possible.**

Christopher Reeve

**IN THIS MOMENT, HONOUR THE FACT YOU SHOWED UP**

# The key is to start small, encourage progress and celebrate small wins.

Greg McKeown

Show up messy,
show up imperfect
but just keep
showing up.

Jenna Kutcher

**The first step toward change is awareness. The second step is acceptance.**

Nathaniel Branden

# It's time to stand up for the life you deserve

# WHEN YOU HAVE A DREAM, YOU'VE GOT TO GRAB IT AND **NEVER LET GO.**

Carol Burnett

**Optimism is the faith that leads to achievement.**

Helen Keller

# All progress comes from tiny wins that gather momentum

You are more powerful than you know.

Melissa Etheridge

> The secret of getting started is breaking your complex overwhelming tasks into small manageable tasks and starting on the first one.
>
> Mark Twain

**There are no wrong turns, only unexpected paths.**

Mark Nepo

100 per cent committed to make goals a reality

**It's all about having that inner confidence.**

Jennifer Aniston

# I'm grateful for everything I have. I'm grateful for it all.

Jennifer Lopez

Release limits and boundaries; embrace potential and possibilities

**LITTLE DROPS OF WATER MAKE THE MIGHTY OCEAN.**

Julia Carney

Do your little bit of good where you are; it's those little bits of good put together that overwhelm the world.

Desmond Tutu

Sometimes success looks like this - collecting trophies - sometimes it's just waking up and putting one step in front of the other.

Mary Earps

**Every moment is a fresh beginning.**

T. S. Eliot

**If you believe it will work out, you'll see opportunities.**

Wayne W. Dyer

EACH SMALL STEP MAKES A BIG DIFFERENCE

YOU HAVE MORE RESILIENCE THAN YOU REALIZE

**Each step you take reveals a new horizon.**

Dan Poynter

**Success is the sum of small efforts, repeated day in and day out.**

Robert Collier

**If you believe in yourself, anything is possible.**

Miley Cyrus

Acknowledge the progress you have made and keep believing in yourself

**Don't be trapped in someone else's dream. Find your own passion and chase after it.**

Kim Nam-joon

# LITTLE THINGS MAKE BIG THINGS HAPPEN.

John Wooden

You can't achieve your dreams if you don't show up to chase them

# It always seems impossible until it's done.

Nelson Mandela

Winning and losing isn't everything; sometimes, the journey is just as important as the outcome.

Alex Morgan

**Fortune befriends the bold.**

Emily Dickinson

# Every win matters – you are doing better than you think

**The future belongs to those who believe in the beauty of their dreams.**

Eleanor Roosevelt

# The difference between ordinary and extraordinary is that little extra.

## Jimmy Johnson

EVERY
ACTION
TAKES YOU
A STEP IN
THE RIGHT
DIRECTION

> I've always done whatever I want and always been exactly who I am.
>
> Billie Eilish

Always remember, your focus determines your reality.

— George Lucas

# The question isn't who is going to let me; it's who is going to stop me.

## Ayn Rand

# EVERY SMALL WIN BUILDS YOUR FUTURE

**Who you are tomorrow begins with what you do today.**

Tim Fargo

**Patience is the key to victory.**

Rumi

# Courageously walk through every door of opportunity

**You don't have to see the whole staircase, just take the first step.**

Martin Luther King Jr

It is often the small steps, not the giant leaps, that bring about the most lasting change.

Queen Elizabeth II

> The great victory, which appears so simple today, was the result of a series of small victories that went unnoticed.
>
> Paulo Coelho

Show up for yourself and choose progress over perfection

## BELIEVE AND ACHIEVE

### Inspirational Quotes and Affirmations for Success and Self-Confidence

ISBN: 978-1-80007-392-0 • Hardback

Supercharge your will to succeed with this pocket-sized dose of dogged determination. There's nothing like a few words of encouragement to help you stay focused while you're on the road to success. This little book is bursting with supportive quotes and fresh perspectives to fuel your journey and strengthen your resolve.

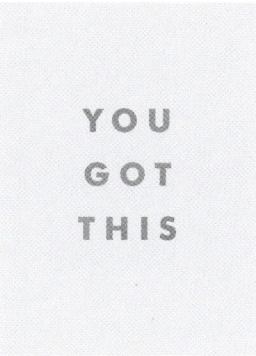

# YOU GOT THIS

## Uplifting Quotes and Affirmations for Inner Strength and Self-Belief

ISBN: 978-1-80007-391-3 • Hardback

Stay fearless and focused with this pocket-sized collection of unshakeable confidence.
If you've got a goal or a dream, never let doubt stand in your way. This little book, packed full of powerful quotes and valuable reminders, is the perfect companion on your quest to conquer your fears and claim your victory.

Have you enjoyed this book?
If so, find us on Facebook at
**Summersdale Publishers**, on
Twitter/X at **@Summersdale** and
on Instagram, TikTok and Bluesky at
**@summersdalebooks** and get in
touch. We'd love to hear from you!

**www.summersdale.com**